TENNIS
SKILLS

FOR KIDS

GARRY POWELL

Wellington

books for kids

Tennis Skills for Kids

Author: Garry Powell
© 2022 Garry Powell
Illustrator: Darya Kazakova

ISBN: 978 1 925308 63 1 (For paperback)
ISBN: 978 1 925308 64 8 (For digital online)

Wellington (Aust.) Pty Ltd
ABN 30 062 365 413
433 Wellington Street
Clifton Hill
VIC 3068

Love this book?
Visit kidzbookhub.com online to find more great titles.

CONTENTS

The 1914 International Lawn Tennis Championship

Jeu de paume *players in 14th century France*

A French indoor tennis court in 1861

Drawing of a lawn tennis court as originally designed by Major Walter Clopton Wingfield in 1874

HISTORY

Games involving hitting balls with your hands can be traced back many hundreds of years.

In France in the 12th and 13th centuries, there was a popular handball game called *jeu de paume*, meaning palm of the hand. Players would hit a ball back against a wall after it had bounced once. A version of this called Downball is played in some schools.

In the 15th century, this game developed into Royal Tennis, which was played by some members of the European elite. The game was played indoors in a theatre, and a ball was hit over a net using racquets. This game is still played in some countries as Real Tennis.

A version of Real Tennis that could be played outdoors was then developed in England in the 19th century. The first outdoor racquets had wooden frames strung with sheep gut. The name changed to Lawn Tennis or tennis as we know it today.

HITTING WITH HANDS

BY YOURSELF

Start with a larger ball (e.g. beachball) and progress to smaller balls such as a tennis ball.

Into the air

→ Drop and then hit the ball into the air using one hand.

→ Hit the ball into the air with the other hand.

→ Hit the ball high and catch it.

→ Hit the ball high, let it bounce once, and then hit it again.

→ Hit with one hand, let it bounce once, then hit with the other hand.

→ See how many hits in a row can you do.

→ Hit the ball up and then again without letting it touch the ground.

Wall bounce

→ Drop and then hit the ball against the wall.

→ Hit against the wall and catch it.

→ Hit with one hand then the other and repeat.

→ See how many hits in a row you can do.

→ Hit against the wall while kneeling, sitting, walking.

Pat bounce

→ Pat bounce the ball with one hand then the other and repeat.

→ See how many hits in a row you can do.

→ Pat bounce while standing still, walking, running.

WITH A PARTNER

Bounce and hit to a partner

→ Bounce and hit to a partner for them to catch.

→ Bounce and hit to a partner — and they return the ball the same way.

→ Do this with one hand, the other hand, and with hands touching together.

Bounce and hit to partner for return hit

→ Do this once, then twice or more.

→ With a partner hit the ball against the wall — let the ball bounce only once and hit the return.

→ See how many hits you can you do in a row together.

Small Circle Ball

This game is sometimes called Hoop Ball, with a hoop used instead of drawing a circle. Partners stand on opposite sides of a 1 metre circle and hit each return bounce back into the circle. The game can be made a contest by playing it to rules similar to those of table tennis.

→ Player A serves the ball into the circle. Player B return hits the ball after letting it bounce only once. A point cannot be won on the serve alone. Player A returns player B's hit, and so on. A point is won when a receiver cannot return the ball.

→ Players take it in turns to have five serves in a row.

→ Only open-handed hits are allowed.

→ The game can be played with the winner first to score 11 or 21 points.

GROUP GAMES

Larger balls are easier to use than smaller balls.

Four Square

A game for 4–8 players.

Court — a square of 2 × 2 metres divided into equal quarters numbered 1–4.

→ One player stands in each quarter; spare players stand on the side.

→ Player No. 4 serves the ball by bouncing it in their own square and hitting the rebound to land in any other square.

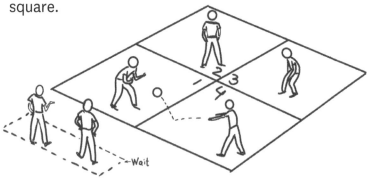

→ The player whose square the ball lands in must hit it into any other square. When any of the four players fails to return hit the ball into another square they are 'out' and move to the end of the waiting line. The new player enters Square 1 and others move around one place.

→ The aim is to get to Square 4 and be the server.

1. The rally (hit after hit) continues until one player fails to hit the ball into another square.
2. If a player hits the ball only to land in their own square they are 'out'.
3. A ball landing on a line is 'out'.
4. The ball can only be hit underhand — with fingers not pointing above the horizontal (no smashes).

Downball

Usually played with a tennis ball. Every hit by a player must bounce before it contacts the wall (a bounce-hit).

A game for 2–6 players.

Played using a wall and a line 1.25 metres parallel to the wall.

Players in an ordered group behind the line.

→ The round starts with player No. 1 serving the ball with one bounce into the wall. No. 2 bounce-hits the ball back in turn, then No. 3, and so on.

→ On the rebound, each player has the choice to let the ball bounce only once on the full before it bounces.

→ The ball must be hit to bounce on the ground only once before it hits the wall.

→ A player is 'out' if they fail to bounce-hit the ball back against the wall, or if their hit lands 'out of bounds' (back past the line).

→ When a player is 'out', they stand to the side, and the next player in line serves to start the following round.

Rules:

1. The ball must bounce in front of the line.
2. The game can be played using one hand or either hand.

Rebound Ball

Played with different sized balls.

A game for 2–4 players.

Played using a wall and a line 1.25 metres parallel to the wall.

Players are numbered 1–4.

→ Player No. 1 hits the ball against the wall from behind the line.

→ As the ball rebounds back from the wall, No. 2 tries to hit the ball back against the wall after it lands. The receiving player can pat bounce the ball until they get into position to hit it back against the wall. But this pat bouncing must be off the rebounding ball, i.e. the ball cannot bounce twice before No. 2 hits or pat bounces it.

→ No. 3 hits No. 2's rebound, and so on.

Rules:

1. On the rebound the ball must land back past the line.
2. All players must hit the ball from behind the line.

Bat or Paddle Tennis

Bat or paddle tennis is similar to Lawn Tennis, but is played on a much smaller court using bats or paddles smaller than racquets.

Players learn basic tennis skills: hitting skills, court craft and scoring. The only thing missing is overhead play of any sort — serves and volleys — all shots must be played from below waist height.

The serve is underarm from behind the base line, and consists of: drop — bounce — hit the ball into the service court. The player at the other end returns the ball after one bounce. The server gets two chances to get a serve into the service court for each point.

Scoring

→ The original French game *jeu de paume* (palm game in English) was played on a court 45 feet long. Players moved backwards or forwards 15 feet after each point was played. In any form of tennis, the winner of a rally gets 15 points.

→ A zero in tennis is termed 'love' from the French *'l'oeuf'* (egg). Each game is started with players 'love — love' or 'love all'. So the scoring may then progress:

→ 15–0 (15–love), 15–15 (15–all), 30–15, 30–30, 40–30. If a point breaks 45, the game is won.

→ If the score is 40–40 it is termed 'deuce' from the French *'a deux'* meaning 'at two' — needing to get two more points in front to win.

→ A set is the sum total of games when one player is the first to win six.

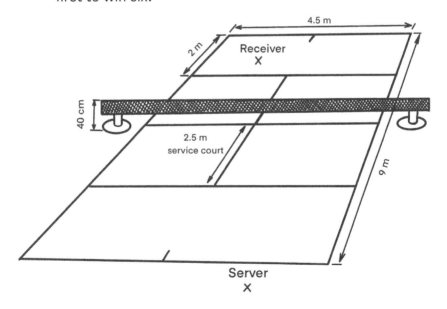

PRACTISE BY YOURSELF

→ Keep hitting — hit the ball into the air.

- ◆ Pat bounce using the bat.
- ◆ Pat bounce into the air.
- ◆ Hit the ball hard into the ground so that it bounces high.
- ◆ Hit up — let the ball bounce only once and hit it up again.
- ◆ See how many hits in a row you can do.

→ Wall hits — hit the ball against a wall.

- ◆ Hit against the wall — one bounce and hit again.
- ◆ See how many hits in a row you can do.
- ◆ Hit against a wall from close up and far away.
- ◆ Volley against a wall.
- ◆ Can you use your right hand and left hand equally well?

TWO PLAYERS

→ Bounce a ball and hit it to a partner who stops it.

→ Hit a ball dropped by a partner.

→ Hit a ball back to a partner who has gently bounced the ball to you.

→ Hit a ball to a partner, and they hit it back.

→ Hit a ball against a wall, and your partner lets the rebound bounce once and hits it back against the wall.

→ Hit to a partner over an obstacle or net.

Eleven Up

→ Serve the ball underhand to a partner, who has to return it after only one bounce.

→ The server wins a point if the returned ball lands outside the named zone, if the ball bounces twice or more before it is returned, if the return hits the floor before the wall or if the returner misses it.

→ Partners take it in turn to serve.

→ Winner is first to score 11 points.

Two Versus One

→ The server stands near the wall and serves into the wall, and either of the others can return hit. The server must hit every other shot, and the other two can hit as many as they like.

→ Once the server loses a point, they are replaced by one of the receiving two, who becomes the new server.

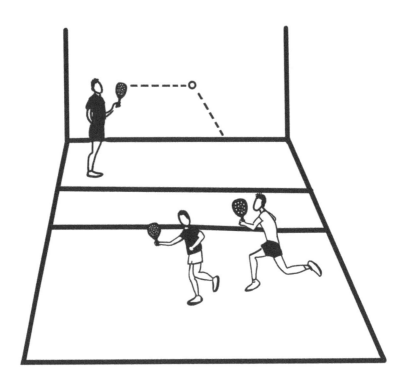

LAWN TENNIS

THE RACQUET

Handle size

'Shake hands' with the racquet
(the Eastern grip). The correct
size is now when the thumb
just touches the first knuckle
of the 'big finger'. The 'pointer'
finger should 'just fit' between

the 'ring' finger and the palm. If the space is too small to
fit 'pointer', then the handle is too thin. If there is a large
space the handle is too big.

The grip

The grip described here is
the basic Eastern grip or the
'starter', illustrated here for
a right-handed player.

Shake hands with the racquet handle and make sure the
'V' between thumb and first (index) finger is on the top.
This first finger is pushed just a little further along the
handle into a 'trigger' position.

BASIC SKILLS

Forehand groundstroke

→ Ready stance — facing the opponent, knees slightly bent, weight on the balls of the feet.

→ Grip — Eastern grip — the racquet held at waist height with its tip pointing forward — non-racquet hand holding near the throat.

→ Watch the ball.

→ Preparation — quick cross-over steps towards the spot where the ball will land.

→ Take-back — an early shoulder turn allows the racquet to be taken back between waist and shoulder height, and the body should be almost side-on to the net.

→ Swing — step forward onto the front foot (opposite to the racquet hand) and swing the racquet forward and upward between waist and shoulder height.

→ Contact — with a firm wrist the ball is contacted before it is level with the front foot.

→ Follow through — the racquet should swing right through up and out towards the net. It finishes over the other shoulder with elbow pointing at the net.

Ready position   Preparation

Swing   Follow-through

Backhand groundstroke

Ready stance.

Determine the direction of the oncoming ball.

Grip — slightly adjust the relaxed 'shake hands' Eastern grip by moving the racquet hand a quarter turn anticlockwise so that the knuckles are pointing up.

Watch the ball.

→ Preparation — push off with the back foot to head towards the ball's landing spot.

→ Take-back — shoulder turn and racquet back early, so that your back is almost facing the target.

→ Swing — step forward towards the ball. Keep the racquet hand close to the body and swing through with a low-to-high path.

→ Contact — the ball should be contacted just in front of the front foot.

→ Follow-through — after contacting the ball, the racquet should continue through outward, across and up.

Preparation

Swing

Follow-through

Serve

→ Ready stance — behind the baseline so that the front foot does not touch the line. The body is side-on to the target with the non-racquet shoulder pointing at the net post.

→ Grip — midway between that of the forehand and backhand groundstrokes (the 'Continental').

→ Watch the ball.

→ Ball toss — weight on the back foot. Hold the ball in the fingers, slowly lift to toss and release the ball upward and out. The fingers are extended with the release of the ball and the hand follows the ball to above head height. The ball should be tossed only as high as the racquet can reach.

→ Preparation — as the ball is tossed, the racquet is smoothly raised behind, higher than and out from your head.

→ Swing — lean forward and swing the racquet through high, to hit the ball at its highest point — ideally when it is stationary, at its peak, just before it begins to fall.

→ Contact — head still — firm wrist at moment of contact — wrist can 'flop' immediately after.

→ Follow through — the racquet should continue its path out towards the net, then down and across to the other side.

Ball toss   *Preparation*

Swing   *Follow-through*

Forehand volley

→ Ready stance — as for groundstrokes but with the racquet held higher so that the tip is at chin height and you can see the ground on the other side of the net.

→ Grip — the 'Continental', as for the serve.

→ Watch the ball.

→ Preparation — step forward and across with the front foot. There should be a very short racquet take-back, only as far as level with the shoulder.

→ Swing — a punch or bump should be used.

→ Contact — with a firm wrist the ball should be met in front of the body line.

→ Follow through — a short follow-through and then back to the ready position.

Ready position

Preparation

Punch

Follow-through

Backhand volley

→ Ready stance — as for groundstrokes but with the racquet held higher so that the tip is at chin height and you can see the ground on the other side of the net.

→ Grip — the 'Continental' as for the serve.

→ Watch the ball.

→ Preparation — step sideways and forward on the front foot so that the shoulder points to the ball.

→ Swing — step into the ball with the front foot.

→ Contact — punch the ball when it is in front of the body.

→ Follow through — a short follow-through and quickly return to the ready position.

Ready position

Preparation

Punch

Follow-through

HARDER SKILLS

Lob

A lob is a shot that can be played backhand or forehand.

→ Ready stance — move to near where the ball will land.

→ Grip — as for groundstrokes.

→ Watch the ball.

→ Preparation — body is behind and to the side where the ball will land.

→ Plant the leading foot firmly.

→ Take-back — shorter than for groundstrokes.

→ Swing — hit under the ball with an angled racquet (open face) while the ball is in front of your position. The swing path is from low to high.

→ Follow through — the racquet should finish above head height.

Preparation

Take-back

Swing

Follow-through

Smash

This is to hit a high ball before it bounces.

→ Ready stance — move to be under the drop line of the ball so that it will drop into the serving position.

→ Grip — as for the serve.

→ Watch the ball.

→ Take-back — take the racquet back so that it is in the serve preparation position — higher than and behind the head.

→ Point at the ball with the non-racquet hand.

→ Swing — as for the serve.

→ Contact — for the serve, when the ball is contacted it should be near its peak and relatively still. For the smash, contact is to a ball that is falling rapidly. The player's aim is to contact the ball at the same height as if it were a serve.

→ Follow-through — down and across.

Preparation   *Take-back*

Swing   *Follow-through*

Half volley

This is to hit the ball just after it has bounced and starting its upward path.

→ Move to the ball and take a low sideways stance (often while moving quickly).

→ Grip — as for groundstrokes.

→ Watch the ball.

→ Preparation — an early shoulder turn and a low, wide stance.

→ Take-back — short, as for the volley.

→ Swing — a blocking movement to meet the ball to the side but in front of the body position.

→ Contact — a firm wrist ensures a solid block.

→ Follow through — from just above court level to waist height.

Approach

Contact

SKILL PRACTICE FOR ONE PLAYER

BY YOURSELF

Forehand groundstroke

Using the forehand grip.

→ Invisible ball
- Hit an imaginary ball to develop a smooth rhythm of footwork, racquet take-back and swing.

→ Pat bounce
- Using the racquet, pat bounce in front of yourself so that the ball gets to between knee and waist high each time.
- See how many you can do in a row, and how many you can do in 60 seconds.

→ Baby bounce
- Pat the ball into the air.
- See how many you can do in a row, and how many you can do in 60 seconds.

→ Bounce and hit
- Drop the ball and hit it against a backdrop — any surface that will not let the ball bounce back (e.g. wire netting, rug or blanket).
- Drop the ball from the face of the racquet, let it bounce, then hit it.

→ Rebound hitting

- Hit the ball against a wall that ensures that it rebounds (brick or concrete). Hit it back against the wall after it bounces.
- Hit the ball back against the wall after it bounces only once.
- How many in a row?
- Hit to score points at a target on the wall.

→ Long and short — hit the ball against a wall from short, medium and long distances.

Baby bounces

Backhand groundstroke

Using the backhand grip.

→ Invisible ball.

→ Pat bounce and baby bounce.

→ Bounce and hit.

→ Rebound hit.

→ Long and short.

Rebound change hits

→ This has to be done at least 6 metres from the wall.

→ Hit the ball a few times backhand and then change to forehand. The key to this practice is to change the grip and foot placement needed to hit correctly.

Alternate hits

→ Hit alternately — backhand, forehand, backhand, forehand.

→ This should start about 8 metres from the wall. To make it more difficult: get closer to the wall so that the changes must be quicker.

Serving

→ **Stance and toss**

- Stand behind a line so that the point of the shoe on the leading foot is 4–6 centimetres from it (this allows a margin of error).

- Stretch your arm and racquet up and out to the height at which the ball will be hit.

- Stretch the fingers to follow the ball and watch it to judge if it gets to the correct height. The ball should land just over the line.

→ **Toss to 10**

- Without a racquet — toss and let the ball drop to the ground. Score a point if it lands just over the line — this would be just inside the baseline of a court.

- Put an object (book, clipboard, towel) on the ground where after a correct toss the ball will land. Only score if the ball lands on this target.

- To make it more difficult make the target smaller.

→ **Invisible ball**

- To coordinate the ball, toss and racquet swing, practise without a ball — toss an imaginary ball, take-back the racquet and swing through gently to hit the invisible ball. This develops rhythm.

Stance and toss

→ **Against a wall**

- Draw a line on the wall at net height.
- Serve against a wall — on the full.
- Serve so the ball bounces once before it hits the wall.
- Change the distance standing from the wall.
- Vary the speed of the serve — slow, medium, fast.
- An advanced practice is to vary the path of the serve — slice, flat, top-spin. This is done by changing the ball toss so that the contact point is in three different positions in relation to the body, arm and racquet.

→ **On a tennis court**

- To practise serving on a tennis court a lot of balls are needed, as there is no return of those that are hit.
- Serve for accuracy — into the corners of the service courts.
- Serve for speed and power.
- Vary the position of serve in relation to the base line — near centreline, midway and near sidelines.
- Practise serving equally into both the forehand and backhand service courts.

→ **Punch serve**

- This is a soft serve so that the player can be sure to get the ball into play.
- Tossing arm in front, and the toss goes so the ball reaches just above head height.
- With a short back swing, punch the racquet through the ball to contact out and in front. Follow through towards the net.

Flat

Top spin

Slice

Volleys

Tennis is one game where it is possible to practise a lot by yourself — a wall can be an effective opponent or partner.

→ Always practise equally on both sides — groundstrokes and volleys both forehand and backhand. Serves to and from both sides of the court.

→ Little hits — stand close to the wall so that the racquet will be only about 1 metre away from it when the ball is hit. Volley against the wall.

  ◆ See how many you can do in a row.

  ◆ Try for 10 forehand and then 10 backhand.

→ Getting bigger — as the skill improves get further and further away from the wall.

→ Draw a target on the wall and volley into it.

→ Volley for speed and power.

→ Alternate — do one forehand and then one backhand volley. See how many you can do without a mistake.

Backhand volley

Lobs

Lob work needs a large open area such as a tennis court, basketball court, oval or grassed area.

A bucket or group of balls is needed, as any hit ball does not automatically return as from a wall or a practice partner.

→ Drop and hit — drop a ball and hit it high over an imaginary object (fence or building). Lob-hit successive balls attempting to land them in about the same spot.

→ Bounce and hit — bounce a ball hard into the ground then lob-hit it high.

→ Lob and return — hit a high ball and run to where it is about to land and hit a return lob from the landing spot.

 ◆ How high do you have to hit the ball?

 ◆ See how many you can do in a row.

Use only forehand — backhand —
any hand — alternate

SKILL PRACTICE WITH A PARTNER

Groundstrokes

These activities should be done with both forehand and backhand equally.

→ Wall hit

- Using only the forehand, hit the ball against the wall and the partner does the next hit.
- Allow any number of bounces.
- Only one bounce between hits.
- Using only backhands, then alternate hands, either hand.
- Keep it up — alternate hits against the wall — how many in a row?
- Follow the leader (against the wall) — the second player copies exactly what the leader does.

→ End to end

- Without a net, hit between partners.
- Any bounces, one bounce, forehand, backhand.
- Increase the distance, decrease the distance.

→ Across a net
  • Any hand
  • Forehand only
  • Backhand only
  • Alternate hands

Serves

When serving by yourself is satisfactory, it's time to try it with a partner.

→ Wall hit — serve against the wall and your partner returns the rebound.

→ Serve and return on a tennis court without a net.

→ Serve and return over a net.

→ Two + two — serve twice into the forehand service court then twice into the backhand court.

→ Target serve — draw or place a target 1 m × 1 m on the court and try and hit it with serves.
  - Change the position of the target.
  - Change the service point on the baseline.

→ Ten up — partners take it in turns to serve. See who is the first to get 10 in.

→ Who is the first to get 5 serves in that the partner cannot return?

→ One to Six o'clock — divide the serve courts into thirds. The forehand court is numbered from 1–2–3 o'clock and the backhand court follows on 4–5–6 o'clock. Serve 'around the clock' from 1 to 6 o'clock. Which section is the easiest depends on differences between players.

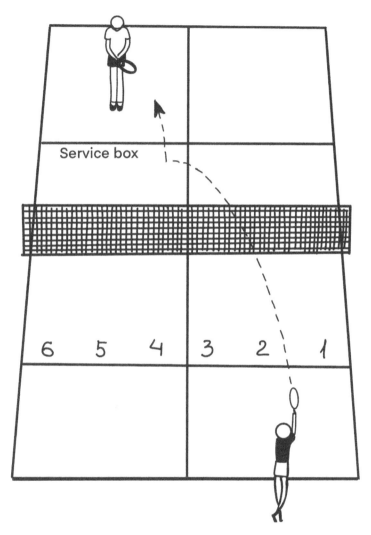

Service box

6   5   4   3   2   1

Backhand court   *Forehand court*

Volleys

The same practices can be used for both forehand and backhand volleys.

→ Throws — one partner has a racquet the other a ball. Underarm throw to the racquet partner who volleys the ball back. A good volley should enable the thrower to catch the return.

- Increase the distance between thrower and hitter.
- Overarm throw to the hitter.
- Do 10 forehand and then 10 backhand.
- Use both forehand and backhand volleys.
- Take turns as the hitter.

  → Wall volleys — throw to the wall and the hitter volleys the return.

  → Both with racquets — one hits against the wall and the partner volleys the return.

  → Net volleys — one throws over the net and the hitter volleys back to the thrower.

  → Change from underarm — overarm throws.

  → Paired hitting — standing about three steps apart, volley to each other.

  → Volley to each other over the net.

Lobs

The same practices can be used for both forehand and backhand lobs.

Take turns as the first hitter.

→ Without a net — lob to a partner who lets the ball bounce and then catches it.

- Lob to the partner who lobs a return hit.
- Using only forehand, only backhand and alternate hands.
- See if 10 in a row be done as a pair.

→ With a net — repeat the same practices as for without a net — lob to catch and lob to lob return.

→ Try to land the ball high so that it lands just inside the baseline.

→ Run to lob — the receiving partner starts inside the service court and has to run back behind themselves to return lob.

GROUP PRACTICE AND GAMES

Relays (4–30 players)

These can be completed simply as rotations, or can be made competitive between teams.

→ **Racquet Bounce** — No. 1 pat bounces the ball while walking around a marker and then hands the ball to No. 2, who repeats this action and so on. When each team member in turn has pat bounced the ball around the marker and No. 1 has the ball again, the whole team bobs down.

→ **Shuttle Hit** — No. 1 hits the ball to No. 2 and then runs across to line B. Number 2 hits the ball to No. 3 and runs across to line A. Number 3 hits the ball to No. 1, and so on.

→ **Cross Hit** — No. 1 hits the ball to No. 2. As No. 2 hits the ball to No. 3, No. 1 runs across to take No. 2's place. Then No. 2 takes No. 3's place, and so on. This rotation continues until all players are back in their starting positions.

Rebound Ball (3 or more players)

No. 1 hits the ball against the wall and then runs to the end of the line. No. 2 hits the rebound back against the wall, then No. 3, and so on.

The game can be played with the rebound having any number of bounces before being return hit, only one bounce (groundstroke), or 'on the full' (volley).

To make the game competitive, an incomplete return hit earns the player one minus point. When one player earns a total of five minus points the game is won by the player/players who have the least minus points.

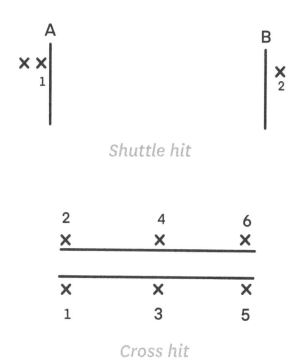

Shuttle hit

Cross hit

Ten Trips (teams of 3)

Three players are in a line about 5 metres apart — each with a racquet but only one ball per team. The ball starts with the middle player B. Player B gently hits the ball to player A, who stops it. Player A then lobs the ball over player B to land close to player C. Player C gathers and gently hits the ball to Player B to complete 1 trip. This routine continues for 10 circuits or trips.

→   Take turns to be in positions A, B and C.

→   To make the game more vigorous and difficult, it can be made progressive. Each player follows their hit to move forward one place. Player B becomes the next player A. Player A replaces Player C and Player C replaces Player B. When all players have returned to their original places that equals one trip.

→   These trips can be done using forehand only, backhand only or any hand.

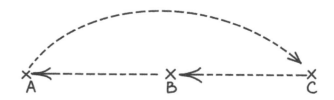

Corner Spry (4–6 players)

Two lines are about 5 metres apart — the leader behind one line and all other players behind the opposite.

→ The leader gently bounces the ball and hits it to No. 1, who stops it and return hits to the leader. Then leader to No. 2, and so on.

→ This practice is always with the leader stopping each return but can be varied by: each player stopping and bouncing the ball before return hitting it or the leader hitting it so the ball bounces once before each return.

→ After one complete circuit to each player, No. 1 becomes the new leader, No. 2 becomes 1, No. 3 becomes 2, No. 4 becomes 3, and so on.

→ When all players are back to their original places, the leader holds the ball in the air to show a finished game.

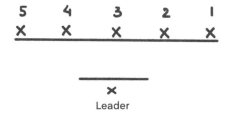

Leader

Over the Top (2–4 players)

This game needs an obstacle as a mid-point — something to hit over. It can be a long bench, a rail, a net (badminton, tennis) or whatever is available.

One-on-one (singles) is played with one person at each end; two-on-two (doubles) has two players at each end.

→ The first player starts the game with an underarm hit over the obstacle (serve). This served ball can be played back either after one bounce or 'on the full'. This process continues (a rally) until one player fails to return the ball. The winner of this rally scores a point.

→ Then the next player serves, and then the next and the next — so the start of each point is served equally.

→ The first to 10 points is the winner.

Keep it Up (4–8 players)

Played over an obstacle or net.

→ No. 1 hits the ball high (serves) underarm over the net to No. 3. After one bounce, No. 3 returns the ball with another high hit. As soon as No. 1 serves the ball they must run in an anticlockwise direction to the other end of the court to stand behind No. 4. As soon as No. 3 returns the ball they run anticlockwise around the net to stand behind No. 2, who by then is hitting the ball.

→ The aim from all players is to get as many hits in a row to score a record.

→ Soft high hits (lobs) should be used as they give extra time to get to the other end.

→ The more people playing the more time for the hitter to get into position at their new end.

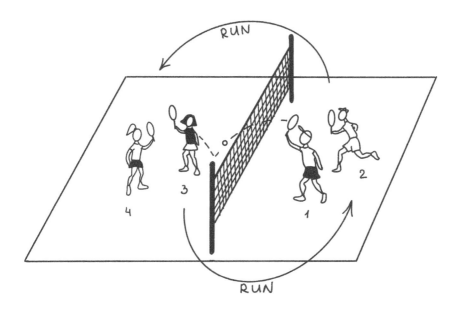

One-bounce tennis (4–8 players)

This is usually played on a full-size tennis court.

The game can be played 2 on 2, 3 on 3, or 4 on 4, with players evenly spread over their end of the court.

→ Each rally is started by a new server using an underarm hit.

→ Any player can return the ball after one bounce (groundstroke) or 'on the full' (volley).

→ A point is won when a team cannot return the ball. The first team to score 10 points is the winner.

Pop-up tennis (4 players)

Played 2 on 2 (doubles) on a full-size tennis court.

→ A player serves the ball underarm. Whichever of the opposing partners receives the serve, they do not hit it back over the net but instead must 'pop it up' so that their partner can. The partner can then return over the net either 'on the full' or one bounce after the pop-up.

→ Any hit over the net can be received either 'on the full' or after one bounce but must be popped up.

→ Either partner can hit any ball except the serve, which must be taken in strict rotation around the four players.

→ A point is scored if a team cannot return the ball over the net or if the serve to start a point lands outside the court.

Paired practices (4–16 players)

→ Many of the paired practices can be safely carried out in a large open area such as basketball or netball courts, football or baseball fields and tennis courts without nets.

→ When these skills are able to be done successfully in such open areas they can then be practised on a tennis court over a net with two players at each end (doubles).

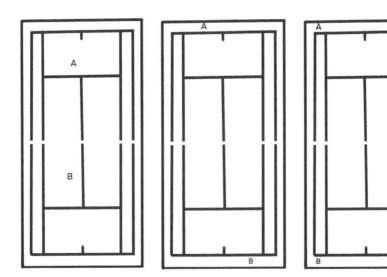

THE GAME OF TENNIS

Tennis is a contest court game where opponents are on opposite sides of a net. It can be played one-on-one (singles) or two-on-two (doubles).

The court size is 78 x 27 feet [23.77 m x 8.23 m] for singles and 78 x 36 feet [23.77 m x 10.97 m] for doubles.

Players hit the ball over the net to try to prevent their opponents from doing the same. Each player is allowed for the ball to bounce only once before they hit it. Then they have to return hit the ball into the opponent's court. When a player fails to return hit a ball their opponent wins a point.

Usually a coin is tossed to decide the server for the first game.

To start a game, the server gets two tries to hit the ball into the forehand service court. The receiving player must let the ball bounce only once before returning it. All other hits can be after one bounce or 'on the full' (volley).

The second point is started with a serve into the backhand service court, and so on. The other player is the server to start each point in the following game.

The aim of the game is to win enough points (at least 4)

and be 2 points ahead of your opponent in order to win a game. Then enough games to win a set — the first player to win 6 games. In junior tennis, one set usually equals one match. In club tennis, most matches are doubles in order to cater for many people.

In adult championship tennis to win a match is to win the best of 5 sets: 3 sets to 0, 3-1, 3-2.

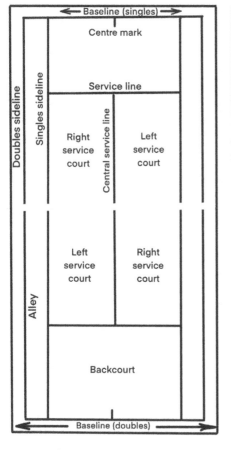
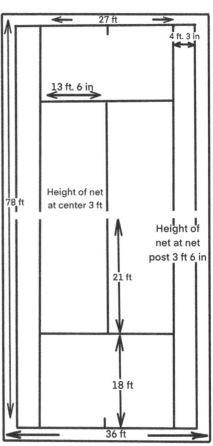

1 foot = 30.8cm

1 inch = 25.4mm

PREPARATION AND FITNESS

EAT TO PLAY

→ Eat regular meals.

→ Eat lots of different foods and food types.

→ Eat for energy — the more you train, exercise and play the more fuel your body needs.

→ Eat only small amounts of sugary or fatty foods.

→ Eat lots of fruits, vegetables, nuts and grains.

→ Drink lots of water especially when exercising.

WARM UP AND WARM DOWN

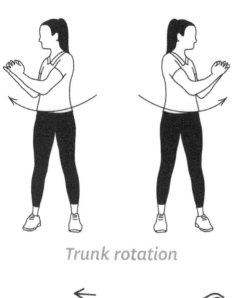

Trunk rotation

Neck

Arm

Inner thigh

Thigh

Calf

Hamstring

Lower back

TENNIS TALK

Ace — when a receiver's racquet doesn't touch a served ball

Advantage — the score of a player who wins a point at deuce (40-40)

Alternate — one hand after the other

Baby bounce — a very small bounce upwards off the racquet.

Backhand — a hit where you reach across your body so that the back of your hand faces the ball

Back swing — taking the racquet back to prepare for the hit

Baseline — the end boundary lines of the court

Bump — a hit with a small back swing, firm wrist and little follow-through

Contact — when the racquet touches the ball

Deuce — a score at 40-40

Double fault — when both serving attempts during one point land outside the service court

Doubles — a match with two verses two players

Drop shot — a soft shot designed to land just over the net

Fault — when a serve lands outside the service court

Foot fault — when a server's foot touches or goes over the baseline before hitting the ball

Forehand — a hit from the racquet hand side of the body

Game — the score when one player reaches more than 40 and 2 points ahead

Groundstroke — a hit after one bounce

Let — when a serve hits the net and lands 'in'

Lob — a high hit

On the line — a ball touching the line is 'in'

Overhead — a hit above the head (serve or smash)

Point — winning a rally

Power — the strength that flows from the player through the racquet and into the ball as it is hit.

Punch — a hit with a small back swing, firm wrist and little follow-through

Rally — a continuous sequence of hits between players

Receiver — the player not serving

Serve — the hit used to start each rally point

Service court — the box part of the receiver's court where the serve must land

Set — the first player to reach a six games total

Singles — a match with one verses one players

Smash — a hard overhand hit during play

Speed — the pace of the ball

Take-back — the backward movement of the racquet before hitting the ball

Tie breaker — scoring in an adult match when the score is six games all

Toss — the throw into the air before the serve

Volley — the hit before the ball bounces (on the full).

Warm down — exercises to help the body relax after exercise or play.

Warm up — exercises to help the body prepare for exercise or play.

Printed in Australia
AUHW020035110422
362109AU00001B/1

9 781925 308631